AN ILLUSTRIOUS NATIONAL SERVICE

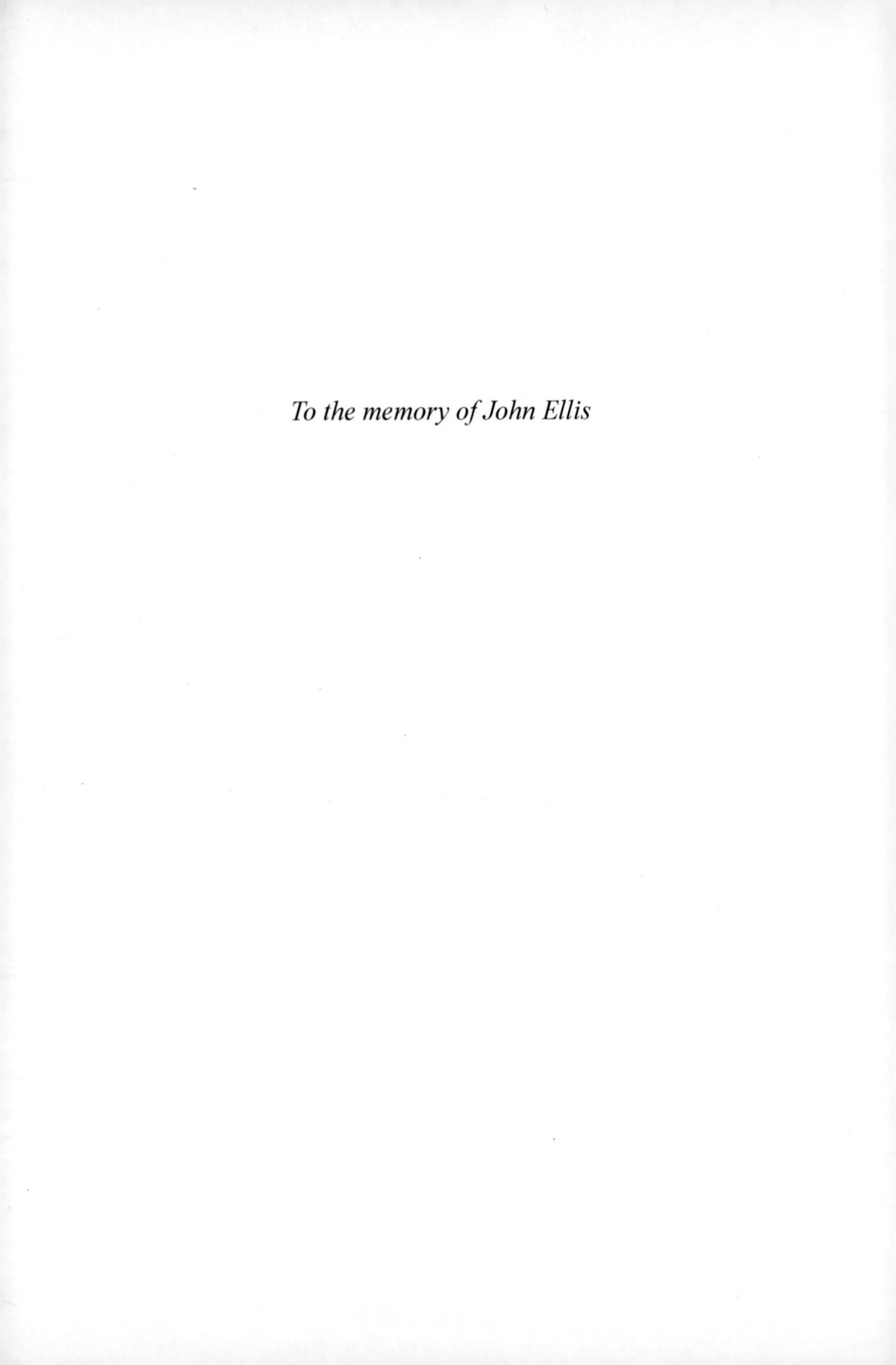

To the memory of John Ellis

To Paul

Best Wishes

AN ILLUSTRIOUS NATIONAL SERVICE

David Woodward

David Woodward

MP

An Illustrious
National Service

First published in 2018 by
Mousehold Press
6, Constitution Opening
Norwich, NR3 4BD

www.mousehold-press.co.uk

Cover design by Jonny Sodah

ISBN 978-1-874739-86-9

Printed by GoWise Print, Norwich

Introduction

Throughout my period of National Service in the Fleet Air Arm I sent numerous letters home to my parents, family, and friends. I did it because I enjoyed writing them. There were, between very active operations on sea and land, other periods of long inactivity. With no interest in playing tombola, or spending time in a pub ashore, I took to writing letters, reading or walking around the local countryside.

Sadly the letters have all, as far as I know, been lost or destroyed. More is the pity. When I felt compelled to write about National Service I decided to use an epistolary form by trying to re-write the letters I wrote some 67 years ago.

But the book is not just about my service. Through the kind help of Diane Coleman and Ann Leftley of the Illustrious Association I have been contacted by a number of fellow shipmates who have subscribed to the content of the book in various ways. I am much indebted to the late John Ellis who died over three years ago He sent me lots of information and photographs. In fact this book would not have been possible without his aid. I wish to dedicate it to his memory.

Vic Smart, a regular seaman, was on the same messdeck as me. He helped me and many others, young National Service ratings as we were, when we came on board. He spoke to me recently about National Service men as being 'marvellous', and so I am glad and grateful to regulars who have contributed to the book.

I have thought long and hard about using at times what I would describe as lower deck language. Do Petty Officers consider themselves lower deck? Some could use the most colourful, vulgar but intense language imaginable. I do not wish to offend the reader and have only given a few examples, but one cannot give a true picture of National Service life without stating how our tutors and instructors spoke to us. Remember, this was at an age when some of my fellow school mates, then in the 6th form, would start the day at school assembly singing 'When Morning Guilds the Skies'. I don't think any teacher ever swore at his pupil. Although some might have done so about them in the staff room.

In defense of the Petty Officers I suffered no harm from their invective, which at times gave me considerable amusement.I would also want to say that generally the Petty Officers in charge of us understood that many of us were suffering from home-sickness. "You're missing your mum and dad, aren't you, son?" And they knew how to help us get over it.

In my case, scrumpy cider helped. I remember a friend who said, "Come on, we'll go and have a drink." I had a couple of pints of scumpy cider and came back and laid in my bunk where I could see the rolling hills of Wiltshire and I thought, "Oh, the Navy is marvellous."

MY OFFICIAL PHOTOGRAPH - AGE 18

HMS ILLUSTRIOUS

Letter to James Payne at Oxford University. He eventually became a clergyman and took the marriage ceremony for Shirley and me, with Rev. Roberts as the local vicar at Worlingham. I was then a Farm Pupil in the Waveney Valley.

MARCH 1948
WAVENEY VALLEY
SUFFOLK & NORFOLK

Dear James,

Pleased to get your letter and to hear you are getting on well at Oxford. So you are in the college rowing eight? A bit different from us rowing to Dunburgh from Beccles on the Waveney.

I told you that I wanted to do my National Service and have volunteered for early call up. I had to go for my medical in Norwich a week ago. Would you believe it I've got into the Fleet Air Arm branch of the Royal Navy? Not many lads are lucky enough to get in but, for once, I overcame my shyness, and persistence paid off.

The medical was a hoot. Dr Sherard from Beccles did it. He's not our doctor, did not know me. It was strange how he talked to the orderly present and ignored me. He was polite and gentle. But as he examined me suddenly said to the orderly, "I plan to write a book about navels when I retire. They all have their own peculiarities," he exclaimed gazing at mine. "I'm sure we ought to learn more from them." I wonder what they would learn from mine.

I told them a lie, said I'd never worn glasses as I knew that would keep me out of the Navy. But I gave my glasses up when I went to work on the farm over a year ago and my sight improved. No more writing School Cert exams.

I was seen after the medical by a recruiting Chief Petty Officer. He made a gesture towards a non-acceptance stamp as though he'd turned me down. Somehow I resolved to let him know I wanted the accepted stamp on my file. With this he grinned and said, "Well done lad – I wanted to be sure you really were set on the Navy. You can become an Air Craft Handler in the Fleet Air Arm. You have been used to being in the fresh air on a farm. You will get even more of that on the Flight Deck of an Aircraft Carrier."

So it's the navy for me soon, I'll miss the farm but have always had a hankering for the Navy so who knows where it might lead?

By the way, I'm sure that the School Certificate I'd got helped. They will have you in the Navy if they think you have enough sense to train quickly. Apparently Air Craft Handlers have to be expert in fire fighting and crash removal.

Look forward to seeing you at Easter if I'm not called up before.

Best wishes,
David

Letter home from where all recruits went for basic training.

MAY 1948
H.M.S. ROYAL ARTHUR,
CORSHAM,
WILTSHIRE

Dear Mum & Dad,

Just to let you know that I arrived safely at Corsham yesterday. There were lots of lads on the train from Paddington on their way to call up into the Navy.

We have been allocated into a big unit for kitting out. There was a bizarre and unexpected greeting. We walked in our civvies from the Naval coaches, with their wooden seats, to the camp, which is like a small town. As we marched through the entrance, veterans of only a few week's service greeted us with cries of 'You'll be sorry.' Not an auspicious welcome. It was relieved by the fact it was a lovely May evening and the sun shone. It was interesting to see the different Wiltshire countryside. The soil is much redder in colour. And the hedges and farm buildings look different.

I was able to soon make friends with a Geordie from Newcastle who shares our small bunk cabin with me and another lad from London. How differently they both speak.

I love the sounds of the camp. The various pipes and calls that echo around the area.

The first call in the morning is reveille at 6.00am. No problem for a farmers boy but some of my chums complain. And the last call at night 22.15 – sorry 10.15pm. 'Pipe Down'.

Another rather emotive procedure takes place at sunset when the flag is lowered.

We have been issued with our uniform; this was done by Wrens in an almost motherly way. We were then given a lesson on doing 'dobeying' – that is washing our clothes – and also how our kit has to be cared for.

We have also been issued with a hammock, a mattress that lays inside and a long thick woollen blanket that will wrap around you a few times. We were taught how to 'sling' this, but for now it is stored away and will go with me wherever I'm posted. But on a shore base we sleep in bunks with grey blankets. No sheets and how I do miss them and pyjamas.

Will write again soon. I'm doing fine.

Much love,
David

James visited my parents when home from Oxford University

JULY 1948
H.M.S. ROYAL ARTHUR,
CORSHAM,
WILTSHIRE

Dear James,

Thank you for your letter. How kind of you to visit my mum when you were home at Whitsun. Her health is poor now, but she seems to be able to make the best of things and often sees an amusing side to life. It looks as though the National Health Service when it fully comes into force will ease the family's worries about the costs of the insulin and other medication that she must have to stay alive. Thank goodness Attlee won the election. Churchill was an heroic wartime leader, but the Tories fought against the National Health policy always. Once in place, though, I do not believe they will have the nerve to destroy it.

Talking of health I have just had four interesting days in the sick bay. It was discovered that I had a bad bout of 'athletes foot'. Now for obvious reasons and the confined quarters you might eventually have at sea they like to nip it in the bud.

Life in the sick bay was glorious. Mainly because besides the three male sick bay attendants we were cared for by three V.A.D nurses. One of them was like a model, tall and slim with such a slender waist. Whilst she was bathing my feet in permanganate of potash I asked her if she would come to the pictures with me in Bath when I got out of the sick bay. She looked rather haughtily at me and replied, "I am afraid I only go out with officers." So that was that!

However the lass on night duty was different. A bit older and a cuddly north country lass. Seeing I was awake in the night brought me a cup of cocoa. She told me she had just got back from weekend leave and got put straight on night duty. Now there are benefits from looking young and innocent. For she said, "If I come and sleep on the side of your bed for an hour or so will you behave yourself?" Of course I agreed and moved right over to the edge and made room.

After a moment or two she said, "Don't fall out of bed – you can get a bit closer". She has said we will go to Bath when I get out of sick bay.

Those four days in the sick bay were enlightening. You were seen by a Medical Officer in the morning and evening. If in bed you had to sit up to attention with your arms folded. The V.A.D Senior Sister was always present and marked on a file at the end of the bed details of treatment. The day before discharge you were issued with a pale blue knee length coat and allowed to walk around the camp. This showed you were deemed sick and not subject to normal camp discipline.

I was glad to get back on the course, however, as if you missed more than four days lectures you might be back-classed and delayed in basic training.

I did speak to one of the medical officers and he was very interested that both of my parents were on insulin for diabetes. "You may eventually get it," he said. "But don't worry, I'm sure that they will advance the treatment for it in your life-time."

I do so hope we will be able to meet up when I have long summer leave in August.

Best wishes,
David

Written to Joe who was Head Horseman on the farm I'd worked on. He was also linesman for the village football team and he kept racing pigeons.

JULY 1948
H.M.S. ROYAL ARTHUR,
CORSHAM,
WILTSHIRE

Dear Joe

Thought I would write and let you know how I'm getting along. How did the football end of season meeting go? Will you still run the line next year? I hope you will still have Pop in goal for another year. But alas, you will not have my sparkling runs down the wing!

I miss the farm a bit but, as we are so busy on the induction course, I don't have much time to dwell on things. Perhaps I miss the horses more than anything. No 'Aldeby Darlin' on the parade ground. It seems funny to have teachers who swear a lot. And to be asked first lecture on Monday, 'Who had a little bit over the weekend?'

But after the talk we had about the dangers of V.D. and then the graphic accounts of how it is treated, I don't think anyone would be 'having a little bit'.

I have been pleased with the way some of the WREN ships company treat the new recruits. Wren cooks were almost motherly when we did galley fatigues. But I have never heard such colourful language from girls.

Those in Writer branch who booked us in on arrival and issued us with Pay Books, under clothes and uniforms, were kind. The lads had to state how many months they were over eighteen. Most were around eighteen and a half. So when I said three days the lovely lass smiled, gave my arm a gentle squeeze and said, "Welcome to the Navy baby."

Have made a few chums in the class and been fascinated by all the different accents. Until now I'd thought of a dialect as being East Anglian. Now I am getting used to all the different sounds. We have got Cockneys, Geordies, Janners, Hebridian, Scousers and Liverpudlians and others. I'll tell you about them when I come home on long summer leave.

I'm learning fast that it behoves well to go with the flow for the time I'm in the Navy. No pun intended. There are so many good things, but it's best to ignore some of the rather gormless ideas that prevail.

For instance, I'm glad that I registered as being C of E (Church of England) when we were asked our religion. No problem for those who were happy to be C of E, R.C. (Roman Catholic) or Free Church, which the Royal Navy called all Methodists, Baptists, Congregationalists and other chapel followers. One rather timid but brave lad insisted he was Plymouth Brethren. "Don't muck about my son," he was told, "get over there with the Free Church."

And a rating who said he was an atheist was booked C of E with the remark, "We'll soon make you a fxxxing Christian."

Life is quite good on the camp. The S.S.A.F.A organisation have a very welcoming hut with comfy chairs and papers and magazines to read. Also they sell cheap coffee, tea and biscuits. It has something like home comfort. We have a lovely view from our hut that looks out onto the rolling Wiltshire hills and grazing sheep. The summer is very hot. And a good thing to as our wash house and heads (naval term for lavatory) is outside. It serves six huts, about 150 lads. The wash basins and showers, although undercover are open a bit to the elements. I'm sure that having just spent a winter working on the farm in bitter weather has stood me in good stead.

Give my best wishes to all the farm chaps and the football team when you see them.

Best wishes,

David

Another letter to Joe; he used to organise trips for vists to speedway races. Bert Spencer and Paddy Mills were riders in the Norwich Speedway Team.

SEPTEMBER 1948
H.M.S. ROYAL ARTHUR,
CORSHAM,
WILTSHIRE

Dear Joe,

I reckon you will be well into harvest by the time I get to the farm and see you all. Have gone down with tonsillitis, and in the sick bay again. But it's been pretty good in a way. Gorgeous V.A.D nurses to look after us.

One of the lads said V.A.D stood for Virgins Awaiting Destruction. I do not agree with that – they are lovely. It's so smashing to have them plump your pillow and tuck you up at night.

It's strange not to be involved in the harvest this year. There is some corn grown round here but lots more grazing land. Sheep everywhere. The countryside is a lot more hilly, and the farm buildings are built different in shape and colour.

No doubt Gillingham F.C have found it hard to get a full team sometimes with the harvest on. A good shower of rain on a Saturday was always handy. But the boss wouldn't think so, would he?

I reckon I'll be home in about two weeks for 10-day leave. See you then.

Best wishes to all the chaps on the farm.
David

P.S. I see Bert Spencer and Paddy Mills are still doing well at the Firs. Do you still get a coach load from the farm? We don't see the Pink'Un at the camp, but they have a Green'un with all the results.
Only a little piece in it about the 'City'.

Aunt Marge (my father's sister) lived 'en famile' with us in Beccles. Until the war came, when she left because of the Blitz, she worked in London in the drapery trade and was for a time a buyer for Bourne Hollingswoth the big Oxford Street store. She was generous.

JULY 1948
H.M.S. ROYAL ARTHUR,
CORSHAM,
WILTSHIRE

Dear Aunt Marge,

Thank you for the postal order. Always handy to have a bit of extra cash when I go for what we are learning to call a 'run ashore'.

What a good idea of yours that I go and visit your great Uncle Bob and your cousin Bertha in Bath. We can get a coach from the camp to Bath only a few miles away. Bertha had got your card saying I might visit next weekend.

I called on them on Sunday afternoon and they made me so welcome. What amazed me was how like dad in appearance Aunt Bertha was. Chiefly because she has what I now realise is a Woodward nose. Also reminds me of Dad a bit because she is a regular church goer and takes a Sunday school. She cooked me some lovely scrambled eggs for tea followed by two slices of home-made fruit cake. When I left late in the evening there were two more slices to take with me.

Dear old Uncle Bob is delightful and so interesting to talk to for a man nearly 90 years old. We got on so very well. He asked me about you all and it grieves me to think that they live so far away that we will never visit them. National Service has done us both a favour.

He is a lifelong cricket fan and supporter of Somerset, who he refers to as 'The Set'. The wireless thrills him so much because, although he can no longer get to the games, he can listen to the scores and results on his wireless. He knows the names of all the players, also of how long they have been with Somerset and each individual's prowess as a bowler, batsman or wicket keeper. He even knows where they field.

It is wonderful to be with a dear old man who is so content. They have told me that I can visit any weekend. I will try and go now and again but will not burden them with a visit every Sunday. Now that the evenings are long I will try to see them for an hour or so perhaps during the week.

Thank you again for the letter and even more so for the postal order.

Love,
David

Oily was the nickname of the tractor driver on the farm, he was paid one shilling (5p) a day extra for this. A very kind man, he helped me a lot when I was a young lad on the farm.

JUNE 1948
H.M.S. ROYAL ARTHUR,
CORSHAM,
WILTSHIRE

Dear Oily,

I wonder how things are doing on the farm. What a good summer we are having. And you will not want a winter like last year.

It is quite an experience in the Navy. I think that I will enjoy it but oh I was so home-sick the first few weeks. I did not think I would miss home so much. But do not tell my folks about it. Poor mum has enough to worry about with her health.

However, I have found the cure. I went to the N.A.A.F.I. club house and had a pint of scrumpy cider. Lying on my back when I got back I felt the Navy was bliss.

We have two different Petty Officers teaching the class I'm in. One of them is a huge but kindly sort of fellow. He gives us lessons on Naval history, how to wash and iron our clothes and uniform. Also he took us one day for an educational visit. We visited the Bristol Evening World printing press on the same day that 'My Love' won the Derby. We waited until the result came through. Then the stop press rolled from the printer and the papers were on sale in Bristol within minutes.

We do not spend any time with our Petty Officer when off-duty. He must have gone through the war and would have much to tell us. Now and again little snippets will come out and I feel relieved I was not born until 1930. I realise that one of the reasons I opted for the Navy was if ever there was another war you would kill or be killed from a distance.

Our other Petty Officer takes us on the parade ground for rifle drill which I have come to enjoy more than I ever thought I would. There is a competition to become the Colour Guard escort for the passing-out parade at the end of our course. Our P.O. is determined to win it. Whereas the other P.O tried to cajole you into getting things right this one is a bully. His language is unbelievable, swearing and colourful. Never heard such oaths – and some on the farm or sale yard could be strong.

Some of the regular recruits are uneducated and a bit dim poor souls. One lad was told by this P.O that if he did not soon grasp things then he would 'come into your billet one night my son and stick my prick into your ear and fuck some sense into you.'

This caused much amusement to the rest of the class but we felt so sorry for the lad. The use of the term 'my son' seemed so inappropriate. No father could ever speak like that. But later I saw him giving the poor lad some extra tuition. Eventually he got there, and mastered rifle drill.

We have quite a bit of off-duty time and there is quite a bit to do without going off the camp. There is a cinema. The NAAFI club is open in the evenings and they come round with a wagon serving tea when we have 'stand easy' break mid-morning and in the afternoon. We also have a 'run ashore' as it is termed, although we're miles from the sea. And you will be amused to hear that all shore bases are referred to as 'stone frigates'. I'll never get used to all the different terms but hope to remember enough to get by.

Give my best wishes to everyone on the farm. I'll come out and see you all when we get summer leave in August.

Best wishes,

David

This letter was written to my parents not long before I had my first long weekend leave.

EARLY JULY 1948
H.M.S. ROYAL ARTHUR,
CORSHAM,
WILTSHIRE

Dear Mum and Dad,
I do hope you are feeling a bit better mum. You have certainly had a bit of a time lately. Am glad that you hope to stay at Southwold in the summer. How kind of Mr Jack Bullard to let you use the hut. It will be more comfortable if the wind is a bit chilly.
I am counting down the days for the long weekend leave we will soon get. Will be home late on the Friday night and do not have to return until the 6 o'clock train on Sunday evening. I miss your Yorkshire puddings mum. I am glad that I'm doing my National Service in the Navy but have decided I will never make it a career. There is much to be said for the comradeship but I'm too much of a free spirit to accept a naval career.

The square-bashing course is going O.K. Our Petty Officer thinks we ought to be selected for the Colour guard at the passing-out parade. I quite enjoy the rifle drill when it goes O.K. Last week I got in a muddle fixing bayonets and cut my hand a bit. But there was a bonus it was bandaged by a most lovely V.A.D nurse in the sick bay.

The commands at drill amuse me. And our P.O. uses the most colourful language at times. "Class will 'Fix Bayonets'. When I say 'Fix' you do not Fix – but wait with it ready. Then when I say 'Bayonets' then you Fix it! Stupid I know my sons but that is the way we do it."

We had a sports day on Monday and I got through all the heats to the 100 yards final and came second. But stupid like they made us run 3 x 100 yards within an hour. I and two other lads came over a bit faint and spent a night in the sick bay. But we still had to sleep in blankets.

Oh how I do miss sheets. Roll on that long weekend.

We have lessons in washing and looking after our kit. Our blankets have to be folded in a special way and laid out at the foot of the bed. Also we had another instruction on the use of oars. We had to sit in a boat on a plinth and used the oars to row in imaginary water. I did very well at this. My experience on Capt. Bloomfield's boats on the Waveney paid off. "Not the first time you handled an oar my son," said the P.O.

We have also had talks on Naval History and very simple English and Arithmetic. So we can understand the basic routine of life aboard ship. It has surprised me how poorly educated some of the volunteer recruits are. Some of them have not read much at all. I realise here how much I owe Peddars Lane school and the Leman School. We also had another talk about the dangers of catching V.D. and the risks we might run from ladies of the night at some of the ports which a ship might visit.

We also have to do duties above the normal class lessons which finish at 4pm: 16.00 hours. I have been one of a 'detail' who were put on the job of mending and repairing beds. On another occasion I was one of the 4 ratings who with a P.O. in charge made up the Corsham Patrol. We were issued with white gaiters and a baton with a metal band at the end. We then marched in single file around the village of Corsham with the P.O. beside, all acting as Naval Policemen to see that ratings on shore leave behaved themselves. Luckily my duty was uneventful. Another time the whole class was put on potato peeling duties at the cook-house of the galley – they don't have kitchens in the navy – they call them galleys.

I'm really enjoying it here in Corsham but can't wait for that weekend leave.

Lots of love,

David.

A letter written just before my first long summer leave.

AUGUST 1948
H.M.S. ROYAL ARTHUR,
CORSHAM,
WILTSHIRE

Dear Mum and Dad,

So sorry that I did not make it when I had given you the dates for summer leave. The night before I went down with a bad bout of tonsillitis. I felt in a complete haze and walked across to the sick bay and the attendant (they call them S.B.A. short for Sick Berth Attendant) took my temperature which was 102F. Next thing I was in the ambulance and on my way to be admitted into the officers sick bay about two miles away. Royal Arthur is more or less closed down for the 10 days summer leave.

I was in a blissful haze for a few days. Could not swallow any food because of inflamed throat. But the V.A.D. sister was so kind and got me ice cream. And I had lemon barley water to drink. Now a week later I feel much better. There is a new drug called M&B which I heard the surgeon lieutenant say was a sulphonamide.

My goodness mum I wish you were getting as much medical care as I am receiving. We in the ward of six patients are seen by a naval doctor every morning and again in the evening. I have one complaint, they have an even greater concern than dad has about keeping your bowels open. On admittance every patient is given a liquid laxative called Black Jack. My goodness it's effective and its action on the bowel dramatic

But after two days normality returned and when asked later if 'bowels had been opened' I said they had. This was on the advice of a Petty Officer patient who told me, to be sure to say "Yes!"

I am now up and about and we walk around the lovely sick-bay garden. The weather is lovely and I am enjoying feeling better. Have been told that I will be able to come on my delayed leave next weekend. It is a blessing that I finished the Basic Training Course before I became ill.

Our class got the top marks. And we acted as the Colour Guard at the passing-out parade. I felt quite proud marching with fixed bayonets behind the Royal Marine band. I am not at all bad at rifle drill. I didn't think that this side of the Navy would appeal to me. But it has a bit. However, I'm glad that side is over.

And I cannot wait to see you all. Will I be home for the Regatta I wonder? Should just make it.

Love as ever – your son,

David

421 Class

A letter to a former Beccles curate who I always sat next to in Church choir. I wrote a lot from the sick bay while I was getting better.

AUGUST 1948
OFFICERS SICK BAY
H.M.S. ROYAL ARTHUR,
CORSHAM,
WILTSHIRE

Dear Rev. Barnes,

I expect you'll be surprised to get a letter from me. But I'm in the sick bay for two-weeks and pass the time writing letters. You always seemed to see the funny side of things when I sang in the church choir in Beccles and I thought this would amuse you.

You may have heard I have started my National Service in the Navy. Soon after enrolling we were all lined up on the Parade ground to be categorised as either Church of England: C of E, Roman Catholic (R.C.) or Free Church ie. Methodists, Baptists, Congregationalists and the like. Now one lad who was a Plymouth Brethren insisted he did not belong to any of these. The Petty Officer, not unkindly, insisted he did not muck about (he used another expletive that rhymes with muck, but I mustn't use such a word to a clergyman) but to get over there with the Free Church lads.

Another boy insisted he was atheist; "Alright my son, so be it. But we'll soon make you a bloody Christian". Having gathered into the various groups, Padres introduced themselves and said they were available if anyone had problems and worries about folks at home we could see him.

I want you to know how much my mum enjoys your visits to see her. She never complains but must feel a lot of pain at times. She was so pleased that the Rector has loaned her a small wireless to have in her room.

Will be home soon on leave. Hope to see you.

Kind regards,

David Woodward

Uncle Fred and Aunt Jenny were in fact Great: Aunt Jenny was my Grandmother's sister. They left London for Beccles during the Blitz

---

LATE AUGUST 1948
H.M.S. ROYAL ARTHUR,
CORSHAM,
WILTSHIRE

Dear Uncle Fred and Aunt Jenny,

It was so lovely to see you again when I was home for Summer leave. It is kind that Aunt Jenny takes mum some of her lovely home-made chutney.

My goodness what a reception I got when returning from leave. Don't tell mum and dad as I don't need them to worry, but I've had to grow up a lot in the past two weeks. When I got back to camp late at night it took me about one and a half hours to find my kit and what my duties were. All my gear was put in store while I was in the sick bay. About midnight I found I was posted to the Barrack Guard which means that we do watch-keeping hours – four hours on, four hours off. But in the time off you eat, clean your kit and get your food at the mess room.

I had to go straight on guard at midnight. You patrol all around the camp which is as big as a small village. We carry a truncheon, wear a white belt and white gaiters. It was quite eerie. Especially as part of my area included the armoury.

At four o'clock in the morning I lay on my bunk, unwashed and worn out and fell fast asleep. About five past eight I was awakened by the Petty Officer in charge of the guard yelling at me to 'get up you lazy young sod – you were absent from your place of duty. Years ago you would have been shot or flogged for that, now you will be on a charge.'

I hurried fearful and dismayed to my guard area. Tired and hungry, I wondered what fate awaited me! But here the almost avuncular kindness of the Petty Officer emerged. He suddenly appeared on his bicycle. He was carrying a flask of cocoa and a large thick scone filled with margarine.

"Get this down you my son – you've missed breakfast I know."

He asked to see me later when he told me he'd discovered that I had only just returned after a spell of sick leave. "You will have to do two weeks guard duty and then you will become the Captain's messenger. As you have got a School Certificate you will not become an Air Craft Handler but will train as a meteorological observer. You will be sent to train at a Naval Air Station in Wales. It is a long course but when you've finished you will either be posted to a weather ship or be on an aircraft carrier."

So it looks as if my short Naval career has taken an interesting turn.

I hope that you and Auntie are doing fine. It sounds a good idea to have your planned new bungalow at Worlingham. Auntie Jenny will be able to pick her wild hedgerow flowers and you will enjoy having your own garden to grow vegetables. Will you still just have brown bread and butter for breakfast?

There is some talk in camp about the new National Health Service. Everyone will soon be having new false teeth and glasses and wigs they reckon. Won't it be a bonus if mum and dad do not have to pay for their insulin they need for diabetes?

When I was in the sick bay one of the Naval Surgeons was surprised to hear both my parents had the condition. He said they will find a cure for it one day. I wonder.

Keep enjoying the plays on the wireless. I hope that I'll be home for Christmas, but maybe I'll spend it on a weather ship.

Love as always,

David

This one was to my parents when I heard I was going to be trained as a Met Observer.

LATE AUGUST 1948
H.M.S. ROYAL ARTHUR,
CORSHAM,
WILTSHIRE

Dear Mum and Dad,

There has been an interesting change in the way things are going. I'm now to train to work on a weather ship. Until I get the posting I'm working as the Captain's Messenger. Such a change – I have to be very smartly dressed and make sure that my uniform is worn perfectly. But it's quite fun. Haven't even seen the Captain. But I sit in a big office with one or two high ranking officers and even better three Wren Officers and about six Wren writers (typists). Then, if any message or memorandum needs to be sent around the station I am dispatched to take it.

What is even more fun I am allowed to ride one of the camp bikes to speed the process. I keep wanting to ask one of the Wrens to come into Corsham or Chippenham to the pictures but cannot pluck up the courage to ask them. Oh, I wish I wasn't so shy.

I expect that I will be home for leave around Christmas.

Thanks for your last letter and the cake. I want to try and see dear old Uncle Bob and Aunt Bertha in Bath this coming weekend. They remind me so much of home. Aunt Bertha makes delicious scones and I love talking to Uncle Bob about the cricket, especially his beloved Somerset. He knows so much about the game. Has taught me the grip for a 'googly'!

Love as ever,
David

Jim was the tractor driver on the farm who I called Oily. I found he did not like this, so I wrote to him as Jim instead.

SEPTEMBER 1948
H.M.S ROYAL ARTHUR,
CORSHAM,
WILTSHIRE

Dear Jim

How are things on the farm? I reckon that you have done harvest by now. It has been a pretty good harvest dad told me when I was on leave a few weeks ago. I wanted to have a trip to the farm but ten days go so quickly. Mum is not very well so time I spent with her was precious.

We soon will be going on to an aircraft carrier to get as they say some sea-time in. It will be for a few weeks and then to a Royal Navy Air Station somewhere. The Naval term for them is 'Stone Frigate'. I'm starting to get used to some of the Naval language. They don't call them lavatories, it's 'the heads'. Also port is left and starboard is right. You don't say 'Yes Sir' to the officers it's 'Aye aye Sir'.

The strangest thing was the few days I spent in the sick bay. When the medical officers come round you have to sit upright to attention in your bed with your arms folded. The care is very good, but they talk about you to each other and the V.A.D. Sister as though it's nothing to do with you at all.

I can see why Naval ratings are referred to as hands. But I do not think deep down they look at us in quite such a detached way. One night a lad was very poorly with some sort of kidney complaint. He was moved in the night to the big Naval Hospital in Haslar near Portsmouth. The Naval Surgeon came and sat with him for over an hour until the ambulance arrived.

They have a very sensible code to show someone is very ill. They are covered with a red blanket. I hope I'll never have one over me.

One or two of the lads try to keep in the sick bay a few extra days by putting their pulse up before it's taken before breakfast. They go to the heads and do press-ups and other exercises to get the heart racing. But it's not easy to fool the V.A.D sister who is like a matron in a civilian hospital.

I'll try to come to the farm next leave.

Best wishes,

David

David Lee *Me* *Geordie Milner*

Still at H.M.S. Royal Arthur waiting to train as Meterological Observer but suddenly this all changed

LATE SEPTEMBER 1948
H.M.S. ROYAL ARTHUR,
CORSHAM,
WILTSHIRE

Dear Mum and Dad,

Would you believe it, everything has suddenly changed again? The powers that be have decided that I'm not to train as a Met Observer. After waiting at Royal Arthur for a posting to the course, it has been discovered that by the time I'd finished a long training course they would only have about two useful months before my National Service finished. I could sign on for seven years, they said.

Well, I thought about this for about a minute and said 'no thanks'. I'll enjoy this life for eighteen months or so I'm sure. But I don't see myself as a regular.

So any day now I will be going to H.M.S Daedalus at Lee-on-Solent and from there to an aircraftcarrier for 6-8 weeks. Rumour has it we may be on the Illustrious.

From there we will go to one of the Royal Naval Air stations around the country. Here again Culdrose is said to be the most likely. That summer leave seems long gone.

Thanks for the many treats you gave me. It was good to taste some Tatterlegs. Fancy brother John going to Hiroshima. He will have lots to tell us.

Love as ever,
Your Son, David.

Tatterlegs –A type of shortbread Mum made from odd pastry bits on baking day

My first letter from HMS Illustrious a day or two after joining the ship at Portsmouth

EARLY OCTOBER 1948
H.M.S. ILLUSTRIOUS
PORTSMOUTH

Dear Mum and Dad,

I am on the Illustrious and so excited. I cannot believe how huge it is. She was in the docks at Portsmouth for the weekend when we went aboard. There were five of us young National Service Aircraft Handlers.

The idea I reckon is that because we've all got a School Certificate it will be easy to train us to move the planes about on the Flight Deck. And to quickly learn the basic firefighting and crash removal techniques.

Oh, but you should see our mess deck. There are three tables down a space about half the size of a classroom. On either side is a long-padded bench that you sit on for meals and to write letters or read. Each member of the mess is allocated his sitting space on the bench.

The leading hand of the mess – I suppose he's a bit like a Lance Corporal in the Army – sits at the head of the table and slings his hammocks above. Then the next two senior ratings are beside him. They are both wartime veterans. One is what they call a 3-badge Able seaman. But the three red stripes on his arm do not denote rank but the years he has served. You see I am gradually learning Naval custom.

The other veteran was in submarines during the war and proudly wears that insignia. We get them to talk at times about their memories. Another rating is coxswain of the Captain's Barge, his name is Victor Smart. He takes high-ranking officers from the Carrier to and from other ships or to the harbour when we are anchored, as we often are, beyond the harbour, or as they say 'in the stream'.

He taught me to sling my hammock and made a stretcher to keep it wide where your head goes. He is a boxer and Middle-Weight Champion of the Navy. He won some big fights.

There are several other interesting lads in the mess. Two or three from London with broad cockney accents. One comes from Yorkshire and another with a real Geordie sound. I find them most delightful if incomprehensible at times. There are quite a few of them in the ship's company.

There is one National Service lad who has become part of the regular ship's company and speaks with a very posh accent. Could be the son of a Duke or something. But he would do anything for anyone. Seems to know some of the officers. And we discovered when he told us he went to 'Slough College' he in fact was an old Etonian. He has a very well fitted Tiddly Suit when he goes ashore. Made, I think, by Naval tailors in London.

Another lad comes from the Shetlands and has a lovely soft Scottish lilt in his voice. He reads a lovely leather bound gilt edged book in his hammock at night. I thought at first it was the Bible but discovered eventually it was a copy of the complete works of Robert Burns.

One of the most fascinating things about living on a ship is it puts you into such close contact with folk who, without National Service, you would never have met. I have been able to live close to someone I have very little in common with and yet been able to see that they are all in fact your shipmates. We all soon find the ones we are drawn to and manage to avoid, as much as possible, the others.

I did find sleeping in my hammock, when I eventually found a billet for it, not the most pleasant environment. There is a constant hum of the ship's working going on when we are at sea. And folk are packed near each other. It is a wonder there are so few arguments. Until now I have seen none of any consequence.

If we've had a busy day on the flight deck we are all glad to relax after a bath. Around 4 o'clock the order is piped – 'Hands to tea and shift to night clothing', which means we have a bucket bath in the tiled room beneath our mess deck. Sailors all keep themselves very, very clean. If you don't take a bath each day and change into a clean shift (underwear) you will soon find yourself hosed down and scrubbed by your mess mates. Body odour is forbidden.

Unless you have requested to grow a beard – which must be a 'full set', like the man on the front of Players cigarettes – then you must be clean shaven.

I tried to get away with a shave every other day and was pulled up coming back from shore leave by the officer of the watch. I was lucky not to be put on a charge. My juvenile and innocent look can be useful at times.

I hope you are both coping OK. Was pleased to hear that Colin and James had paid you a visit. Fancy James going to be a parson. Perhaps he'll marry me one day. I hope he never loses his taste for a pint of best bitter. No doubt dad will have been busy with the farm auctions. It will be the first time I've missed Beccles Horse Sale!

It looks as if I will be home at Christmas. Get the turkeys in the backyard nice and fat.

Love as always,

David xx

Letter to Mr Alec Gill, a local dairy farmer who had a retail milk round in Beccles. I used to go with him on a Saturday morning to hold the pony, while he collected the money.

OCTOBER 1948
H.M.S. ILLUSTRIOUS
PORTSMOUTH

Dear Mr. Gill,

No doubt you have heard from Mum and Dad that I am in the Navy now. Since last month I have been at sea on an aircraft carrier, HMS Illustrious. And I am pleased to say I am part of the ship's company. We have a number of National Service men on our mess deck. One of them is David Lee whose family live near you in Worlingham.

The ship is the training and trials carrier of the home fleet, so there are often exiting and interesting events taking place. David and l work on the flight deck so we are close to events! I have seen landings by test pilots during trials.What skill and bravery they have.

Also we go regularly to the Moray Firth in Scotland where our pilots fly out from Lossiemouth and do their first attempts at landing on a carrier – often with dramatic results.

We have all had to pass exams in firefighting, crash removal, and moving planes speedily on the flight deck.

Thank you so much for your kindness to my parents, I hear they recently had a sack of your spuds. No doubt you will have finished haymaking, and harvesting. I wish you sunny days for getting in the sugar beet.

I will try and visit when on leave. I expect Kitty the pony is getting ancient now, but I know you had a lovely bay cob to take her place on the milk round.

With all best wishes,
David

P.S. Remember me to the two Miss Gills who work in the dairy.

Colin Baker was a long standing friend. We were both at Sir John Leman school in Beccles. He went on to have a distinguished career in the Colonial Service. Years later we were to write a book together about our school days.

OCTOBER 1948
H.M.S ILLUSTRIOUS
PORTSMOUTH

Dear Colin,

Good to hear from you and I am very pleased that things are going well at Birmingham University.

You asked in your letter what do Aircraft Handlers do on a carrier. Well, in a way we are flight deck labourers. We move the planes about, literally pushing them from the hangar to the flight deck, folding the wings. Flight deck work can be – well not exactly frightening, but I find myself thinking, 'my God, you've got to be bloody careful here, boy.' When a squadron is taking off, everyone on the flight deck has to manage the chocks. You lay under the plane, holding the chocks while the planes rev up, till they take off. The slipstream from the revving planes! That's the only thing I don't like doing.

But one of our Petty Officers told us that if it wasn't for us no plane would be able to land or take off. In fact, I have been made aware that we are part of a team, in which we all play a part. And I'm proud to be a member. So here is what we do.

In the first instance we all had to get through a short spell of training. All National Service men I believe had to have a school certificate to join this branch. We are divided into teams that work in different parts of the flight deck. I and David Lee are in a team at the fo'c's'le port side of the ship. Or, in landlubber's terms, at the front on the left. We move the planes on to the flight deck, and then put them in position for take-off.

We have to answer to the command of the Petty Officer. A

leading hand works with each team.They are older regulars and have seen wartime service. Lt. Commander Filmer is in overall charge.A wonderful man.

Some of us handlers on National Service have special duties. There are the Hook men – two men, one on the port and one on the starboard side who run out and release the plane from the arrester wires across the flight deck.

Another man has the responsibility of watching the plane coming in to land, through binoculars. He reports to the batman advising him the landing plane has its hooks, its flaps, and its wheels down, ready for landing. The batman, by the way, is an older skilled pilot – a Fleet Air Arm Officer.

Then there are the Fearnought suit men. They are dressed in asbestos suits and helmet and visor and they go in to rescue anyone trapped in a plane on fire. I have seen some heroics.

On a few occasions I was called to help a special photographer who came on board to take pictures of planes during special sea trial. Holding a lamp for him as the plane approached and landed. I was not privy to what it was all about, of course. But it was fun.

It seems a lot to tell you, Colin, but I hope I have given you an idea of what Aircraft Handlers do. Here's a photograph of us moving a plane on the flight deck.

Thank you so much for going to see Mum. I know how much she loves to see you. Doesn't she have a good sense of humour.

I hope we can meet up soon.

Love to you and all the family.

David

Scenes from the flight deck

088

Mr Knights was a tenor in the church choir when I was a choir boy. He owned a Waveney One-Design sailing boat, and every Sunday afternoon I used to crew for him.

OCTOBER 1948
H.M.S. ILLUSTRIOUS
PORTSMOUTH

Dear Mr Knights,

I hope you remember me. During the war I was your crew in sailing races on the Waveney at Beccles, in 'Picarty', your Waveney One-Design.You used to pay me with McVities biscuits for my crewing duties.

You will be surprised to learn that I am now doing National Service in the Royal Navy. I am on the aircraft carrier H.M.S. Illustrious. Have you ever seen an aircraft carrier? It is huge. There are nearly 1400 in the crew – not just the one you had. It makes the paddle steamer that used to take us from Lowestoft to Felixstowe seem like a canoe.

I joined the ship at Portsmouth harbour last October. When a ship leaves harbour, unless on ceremonial occasions, they clear the lower deck of all ratings. When we were ordered up to the flight deck, the ship in the middle of the ocean seemed as small as we did in your sailing boat on the Waveney. It made me wonder if size isn't all relative.

How are things going with you and your family now the war is over? I trust the biscuit business is flourishing without the wartime restrictions. And it seems to me that there are many splendid things going on. Folk in the majority of cases are all looking out for each other.

I would love to meet you again sometime when I'm on home leave.

My very best wishes to you and Mrs Knights .

Yours sincerely,

David Woodward.

Letter to Joe, well known for his racing pigeons.

OCTOBER 1948
H.M.S. ILLUSTRIOUS
PORTSMOUTH

Dear Joe,

How are you getting along, bor? I trust those racing pigeons of yours are getting home on time.

What do you make of this picture of us shipmates painting the Illustrious? A lot of us are supposed to be aircraft handlers but, as you can see, all we are handling here is a paint brush. I have marked on the picture where I am. It really is fun and there's nothing to worry about, because if you did happen to slip all you would do is fall in the briny. They soon get you fished out. We are in dock so they could easily do that.

Some of the Petty Officers walk along the side of the dock and shout out and tell us any bits that have been missed. They call those bits 'holidays'.

I wonder how poor old Mr. Rackham is. I don't think he would cope with this. He never did like topping up a haystack at harvest time, did he? I remember he used to say he couldn't do with heights as he got older. I think you used to do that for him, didn't you? What about this - how would you fancy painting a ship?

I am not sure when I will next be on leave but I promise I will come and see you if I can.

My regards to everyone.

David.

Painting the ship

PORTLAND NAVAL DISASTER:

H.M.S. Illustrious launch sinks in gale

ONE MIDSHIPMAN and 28 ratings from H.M.S. Illustrious are feared to have been lost when a liberty launch in which they were returning to the aircraft carrier sank in last night's gale.

THE LAUNCH, which had left Weymouth Pier, was close to the carrier in Portland Harbour when the disaster occurred, and it is believed she sank immediately. Search for the survivors was made by Weymouth lifeboat and naval craft and it is stated 21 men were picked up.

The launch, which was taking naval personnel back to the carrier, left Weymouth late last night in the teeth of a south-westerly gale. Visibility was at times reduced almost to nil in blinding rain squalls.

She sank inside the harbour, but the cause is not yet known. It is possible she struck a buoy or floating wreckage.

A midshipman was picked up unconscious, but died later. It is understood he was the coxswain of the launch.

Weymouth lifeboat was called just before midnight and made a search of the breakwater for possible survivors, but her crew recovered only a number of lifebuoys and two naval greatcoats. Search was still being made in the harbour today.

NO SIGN OF A LIVING SOUL

The coxswain of Weymouth lifeboat (Mr. H. Palmer) said, "We left harbour at a quarter to twelve. The weather was

29 FEARED LOST

very bad – blowing a gale . We reached Portland Harbour at about midnight. We had a message to proceed to the aircraft carrier Illustrious, and they told us to search the breakwater for men who might have clambered there or might be clinging to the rocks. We searched from end to end.

"Searchlights were played on the scene by near-by ships, but there was no sign of any living soul.

"I decided to land three men on the breakwater and they made a thorough search.

SANK NEAR CARRIER

"We recovered a number of lifebuoys and pieces of wreckage. I reported to the Illustrious and put some of the wreckage aboard there. Then we resumed the search and went along to the boats and searched around them. In fact, we went everywhere we thought might help in the search.

"Altogether we found 10 life-buoys, and it is possible some of these were thrown over from the Illustrious, as we understood the motor launch foundered somewhere in her vicinity.

"It was a very wild night. The seas were just a mass of foam and I don't think any man could live in it for long."

TOWN'S SYMPATHY

News of the disaster was brought to Weymouth Town Council at their meeting to-day by the Mayor. A message of sympathy has been sent to the Commanderin-Chief.

Dorset Daily Echo and Weymouth Dispatch (October 18, 1948)

Letter to James, still studying at Oxford

NOVEMBER 1948
H.M.S. ILLUSTRIOUS
PORTSMOUTH

Dear James,

I wonder if it's because you are half on the way to being a clergy man and used to preach as a young man at the mission room that I'm writing this letter to you. I cannot bring myself to worry Mum and Dad with the details of events on the ship in October. We soon had a baptism of sea life. You may have read in the papers of the Liberty boat tragedy on the Illustrious.

A boat bringing ratings back from shore leave capsized in Weymouth beyond the breakwater and 29 sailors were drowned. Ironically I was on that same boat the night before and I thought what a rough trip we had. But never that the bloody thing might sink. Sorry for the language Jim. But swearing abounds now.

Two from our mess table were lost. It was so hard to sit and go through all their belongings. Our leading hand did it in the most gracious manner – but it seemed to me an invasion of their privacy to read through their last letters and the like. But it had to be done to know who to write to, girlfriends, parents etc.

I believer our Commander, Richard Courage, contacted them all. I have heard from older ratings what a fantastic man he is. He has come over on the ship's tannoy in the Dog Watches to give us a report on how the survivors picked up that night are getting on in hospital.

The episode has brought us all closer together. One chap on our mess – a tubby little Yorkshire lad, a great churchgoer – reckoned the Lord saved him as a piece of wood debris from the sinking ship was washed near him as he struggled in the water. He clung to this until rescued.

I wanted to ask him why the Lord didn't choose to save them all. But it would have been pointless and cruel. He is a dear chap and speaks ill of no one. One of the older men drowned was a veteran diver who had gone through the war, no doubt seeing action on various ships. How sad after coming through all that to lose his life in such a tragic accident.

On a more uplifting note I have been made aware how much music plays such a tremendous leavening on our emotions. There was a memorial service at Weymouth Church for those 29 sailors lost in the accident. The whole ship's company were present. The families of all those lost sat in the front pews of the church. Some of the lads who died were young National Service men. The Last Post was played and a lump came to my throat and a tear trickled down many cheeks. A silence followed. Then the strains of the Reveille from the Royal Marine Buglers filled the body of the church with its uplifting calls.

Even the grieving parents and relations somehow managed to stand tall. Since then, music will always play such a part in my life. Never again will I hear those notes without that day coming to mind.

Grief is always made more bearable I'm sure with suitable music at the time. These events have made me realise how stupid it is to waste time on needless matters and arguments.

I have also realised that the Royal Navy is going to help me grow up. And quickly too.

Look forward to seeing you on my next leave. We have heard we may go to Gibraltar before Christmas.

With all best wishes,
yours sincerely,
David

Many a brave heart lies in the Deep

While laying in bed, wild winter nights–it often occurs to me
To try and picture those dear ones–bereaved by the toll of the Sea.
'Tis one of these fatal occasions–I'm writing about to-day
The story of Boys from the Illustrious– anchored in Portland Bay.

The Boys that helped to make her crew–were on her quarter deck.
All spick and span was every man– the smartest ever met
Waiting for the Liberty Boat–to take them to the shore.
To have a little fun of course–away from drill and bore.

At last the Boat arrived with them–all safe at Weymouth Pier
They all dispersed to different parts–they left there with a cheer.
The wind blew such a raging gale–the night wore sadly on
My thoughts strayed to those sailor-boys all happy in the throng.

I little knew that duty–would call them back that night
But those brave souls all ventured forth with hearts so gay and light.
To make their way back to the Pier through all that wind and rain
To board that fateful Liberty Boat–to take them back again.

Lines composed by Jack Pitman

The wind still blew a raging gale–as she cast off from shore
Those Boys in blue were happy–not knowing what was in
store.
Once out in the Bay she rocked and rolled–the Sea it was
so rough
Those sturdy Lads did take it tho'–'cause they were pretty
tough.

She steamed towards that mighty Ship–that wild October
night
The rough sea lashed against her sides–the Boys were
clinging tight.
When all at once the boat capsized and sank beneath the
waves.
Those Boys in blue were struggling hard–their dear young
lives to save.

But God had willed it not to be–alas–it was their time
And so below they're sleeping–they numbered twenty-nine.
The Weymouth lifeboat put to Sea–in all that wind and rain
To search for those poor Sailor-boys–but proved just all in
vain.

And so dear friends those Boys were lost–it was a tragic blow
To mothers, wives and sweethearts–and it only goes to show
That we who are alive and well–should offer up a prayer
For those dear lads in Navy blue–asleep in the deep some-
where.

Now this is the end of my story–my aim I'm sure you'll agree
Is to raise some funds for those dear ones–bereaved by the
toll of the Sea.
Please buy this little Poem–your patronage will show
That you have done your duty–to those who're sleeping
below.

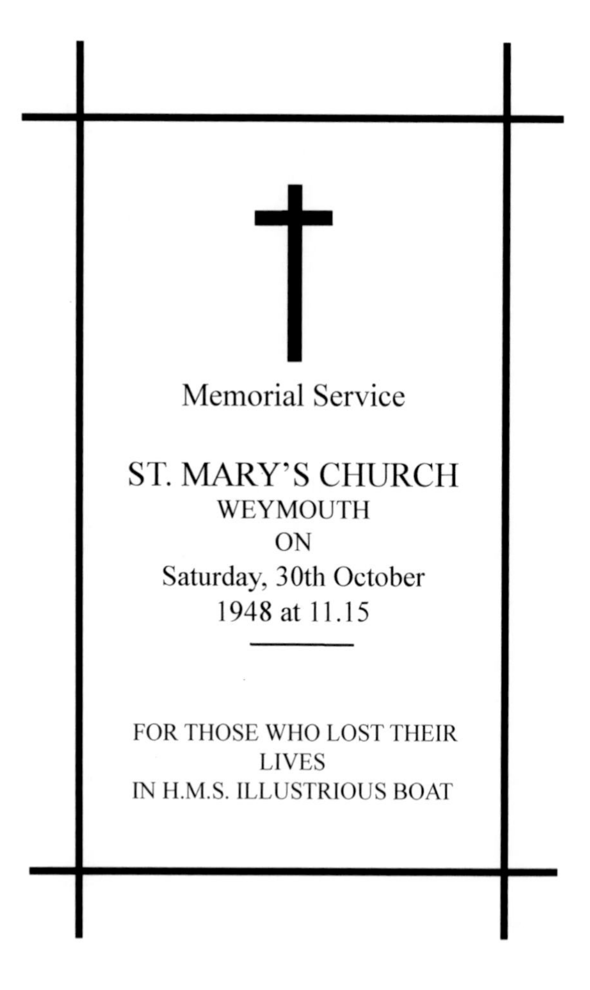
Memorial Service
ST. MARY'S CHURCH
WEYMOUTH
ON
Saturday, 30th October
1948 at 11.15
FOR THOSE WHO LOST THEIR
LIVES
IN H.M.S. ILLUSTRIOUS BOAT

Letter home

DECEMBER 1948
H.M.S. ILLUSTRIOUS
PORTSMOUTH

Dear Mum and Dad,

Thanks for your long letter mum, pleased to hear that you are feeling better and the leg is responding to treatment. Fancy both you and dad having to have insulin injections every day. Thank goodness we have got the new National Health Service to help.

I can tell you about an amusing incident. I nearly lost a piece of my ear the day Prince Charles was born. I had gone for a haircut and was half way through the trim up when a saluting gun was fired. Now the barber's shop was very near the gun sponsor and the barber nearly jumped out of his skin and the scissors clipped my ear! Lost a speck or two of blood. A styptic pencil soon put matters right.

It won't be long before Christmas. Cannot wait to be home for a spell.

Love as always,
David

With Best Wishes for

Christmas and the

New Year

With Love

From David

John Ellis *Vic Graham*
the Hookmen

Letter to Mr. A. Rackham, foreman at the farm, in Norfolk, where I worked until I joined the Navy.

WINTER 1949
H.M.S. ILLUSTRIOUS
PORTSMOUTH

Dear Mr Rackham,
I hope this letter finds you in good health. Do you recall that during that long winter last year you told me that in all my life I would never have to put up with any colder weather. It was certainly cold: the river Waveney was frozen solid and people were skating all the way down to Oulton Broad. On the farm we had to break the ice on the 'Hoss pond' so there was water for the stock to drink. We carted straw into the yards for thick bedding and we had to keep the hay racks full. We even had to take the churns of milk in a tumbril across several fields to be picked up near the Gillingham Village Hall. Snow had drifted, blocking the roads to the farm.

Well, Mr Rackham, I have now been somewhere even colder. HMS Illustrious, the ship that I'm on, has been north of Bergen and into the Arctic Circle. We understand that trials are taking place to study the effects of such very cold conditions on flying on to an aircraft carrier.

My goodness it is colder than it was in the Waveney valley in 1947. If you just spit, it has frozen by the time it hits the deck. Many of the National Service lads are saying we are lucky to be on a ship carrying out these trials in peacetime. Whatever must it have been like on those ships on the Arctic convoys during the War? Then it was not just the cold, but the risk of attacks from U boats and enemy bombers.

Please give my best wishes to everyone on the farm. I will try to get to see you all next time I am on leave.

Kindest regards, Sincerely

David Woodward

Another letter to James

MARCH 1949
H.M.S ILLUSTRIOUS
PORTSMOUTH

Dear James,

Will you tell Mum and Dad when you see them next of the contents of this letter, but cut out the bits that might make them worry when there is no need. It's useful to have someone like you to write to and be able to get things off my chest.

I've had another spell in the sick bay but this time aboard a ship. Quite different. Missed the V.A.D.s with their slim waists and the chance now and again to have a cuddle.

We have three S.B.A.s (Sick Berth Attendants). One is a chief in charge and a Petty Officer. They both sleep in a small berth with two bunks. Officially it is for sick Officers but they are mostly treated in their own quarters.

All of the attendants are very kind and gentle as nurses. I had to go in the sick bay as a huge carbuncle came up under my arm, the pain was terrible. They took me in at once and called the Surgeon Lieutenant. Within ten minutes it had been lanced. Oh, the relief.

They found I kept running a high temperature, so I was put into one of the eight bunks on the bay. Have been in over a week and am writing from there now I feel better...

In a way I have seen as much action in here as on the flight deck., Albeit much different.

Our bunks are one above another. I'm in the lower, with a big burly Colour Sergeant of Marines above. Poor chap had an ulcer and was waiting to be taken ashore to hospital. We get on very well now, after a rather inauspicious start to our first night together in the sick bay. It was a pretty wild night in the Irish Sea and waves were breaking higher on the carrier than usual.

Suddenly the seals on the scuttle near my bunk burst and water gushed through, soon leaking down on to the poor slumbering Colour Sergeant.

The sudden soaking awoke us both, "Have you just pissed yourself?" the Marine yelled out, "I'm getting wet and it's dripping down from your bunk."

He called the S.B.A. on duty who quickly moved us both. The Marine walked to another area of the Sick Bay and the attendant gave me a piggy-back to the bunk above him, as I was not deemed well enough to walk.

Once settled the Sergeant's demeanour changed and he enquired, "You alright son?" He must have been at least in his mid-thirties but we had quite a good time and enjoyed having a yarn, reading the paper and listening to the wireless. It was near St David's day and there was a lot of lovely Welsh singing.

With all best wishes,
yours sincerely,
David

Three mess mates in the Mediterranean

Another letter to Joe. Aldeby Darlin' was a very steady and gentle mare, and so reliable. Kathy was a former hand-girl.

APRIL 1949
H.M.S. ILLUSTRIOUS
PORTSMOUTH

Dear Joe,

How are things on the farm? No doubt you have been busy drilling. Does old Rackham still use Aldeby Darlin' on the Smythe drill for the sugar beet? I bet he is happier to have Kathy following the drill rather than me.

We have been doing some trials of night flying. It is strange and rather eerie. As aircraft handlers we go in a group with our Leading Hand and Petty Officer on the fo'c'astle lift.

Once on the flight deck we have to stand for a few minutes for our 'eyes to become accustomed to the gloom' as the Petty Officer puts it. I'm quite amazed how caring he is of us lads. As long as we follow his orders all is well.

It is surprising how soon what once looked like a black night soon becomes like a dimmed version of day light. When the clouds break so the stars shine through it is even better. The senior flight deck crew use illuminated wands to direct the planes forward to us as they land. I think there were only three Fireflies with very skilled and experienced pilots on these trials. As far as we could see the landings were all perfect. I do not know if it was planned that way but the few times we have had night flying trials the weather has been perfect with a good moon. And there is a bonus; the next afternoon we get a make & mend, so we rest, read and do any dobeying required. Hope all is well with you. Give my best wishes to everyone on the farm.

Kind regards,
David

Letter home

MAY 1949
H.M.S. ILLUSTRIOUS
PORTSMOUTH

Dear Mum and Dad,

Thanks Mum for another lovely cake. Lots of the lads on our mess get one and we always share them.

I have talked to my friend Peter McKinnon and he has advised me to stay on board at Bank Holiday weekends. I hope you won't mind. In future, I'll come a bit later, on a Ten-day leave.

Peter tells me that life is very relaxed on board at this time. There will be no flying duties, but we do still have to look smart in our Tidley suits. Mine has been refitted by one of the ship's tailors. Boats bring visitors out to look around the ship, so it will be good fun showing them around. Especially the local girls.

Peter is a good friend and has a very important and dangerous job on the Flight deck. He and I have set up a small business together, scrubbing hammocks for other ratings. He has access to a narrow passage around the ship's island. This gets very hot so they dry quickly. For health reasons, hammocks need to be kept clean, and at sixpence a go we are not rooking our mess mates.

The ship recently made a courtesy visit to Torquay. A party of us, including the leading hand on our mess deck, were invited ashore. The leading hand is a regular who served during war time. We were invited to have tea with the Mayor and his family. His oldest daughter had just been crowned local Beauty Queen.

Later the leading hand took her to the pictures. In Torquay, they let sailors into the cinema at reduced price. We paid for the cheapest seats and then were allowed to go in the best. If we go to a local cafe, the prices are also reduced.

However, it's not like that everywhere. At regular ports like Portsmouth, or Plymouth and the like, sailors are never made so welcome. I am looking forward to Navy Days and after that a Ten-day leave at home.

My love as ever,

Your Loving son, David

Another letter to James

JUNE 1949
H.M.S. ILLUSTRIOUS
PORTSMOUTH

Dear Jim,

Once again I write to pour my heart out to you. But before that, I trust that now your National Service in the RAF is over your studies at Oxford are going well. I have heard that you were able to bring a lovely Border Collie home from the air station you were at, and his name is Radar. That sounds very apt. Your mum tells folks she loves taking him out on the common.

There has been a lot of activity on the ship.The flying trials bring much excitement and interest. I have been to parts of the world I never thought l might visit: Ireland, Wales, Scotland,The Azores, and even the Arctic Circle north of Bergen. But as we are part of the Home Fleet, we will not get as far as my brother, John, who recently was sent to Hiroshima. The devastation he saw there he finds hard to talk about.

Sometimes an event on the flight deck shakes us all up. Not so much at the time, but afterwards, when perhaps you're dozing off in your hammock. There was a dreadful crash into the barrier recently. The plane, a Seafire, turned over, then burst into flames.The impact was explosive. I had never before been so near such an event. Under our Petty Officer my team of Deck Handlers got the foam hoses into action. But the Fearnought suit men bravely went in to rescue the pilot. In their asbestos suits they lay round him until the foam spray had subdued the flames.The pilot was saved, but had some burns. So did the rescue boys.We have been told that they have been recommended for medals.

So you see, Jim, l am growing up fast, but would not miss the experience and comradeship we share.

My love and best wishes to you. I trust it won't be long before we are sharing a pint. We will have much to talk about.

Love to you,

David

R.A.F. WEST RAYNHAM

JULY 1949
H.M.S. ILLUSTRIOUS
PORTSMOUTH

Dear Mum and Dad,

Would you believe it I'm coming to Norfolk, to the Royal Naval Developent Unit, which is based at R.A.F. West Raynham. It's a huge establishment near Fakenham.

I think I may have told you we have a chap called Peter Nobby Noble on our mess deck. Ever so posh but ever so nice. We were chatting one night, him and my mate, David Lee, and I mentioned that you had been very poorly and that we were never able to get home to Suffolk on weekend leave. Now, Nobby went to Eton, the top school in the country. He knows one or two of the officers and their families. He must have had a word or two with the powers that be and I will soon be nearer home. Even in the Navy its not always what you know but who you know!

I will be really sad to leave Illustrious as I have made so many lasting friendships. But it will be good to see you all more often. Also I'm glad David Lee will still be with me. He wants to see more of his mum, I'm sure, now that she is widowed.

No doubt we will spend a few nights at H.M.S. Daedulus in Lee-on-Solent on our way to West Raynham. The Navy never does it the simple way of moving you straight from one base to another, but I expect they have sound logistical reasons for this! Give my love to Aunt Marge,Uncle Fred and Aunt Jenny. Tell Mac I'll be able to take him on the common for a run more often.

Your loving son,

David

Refuelling bowser alongside a Vampire

Another letter to Colin Baker

AUGUST 1949
H.M.S. HORNBILL
RAF WEST RAYNHAM

Dear Colin,

I cannot believe my luck. David Lee and I have got a posting to the Naval Air Development Unit at West Raynham.

You cannot comprehend how the last few months of my National Service will be compared to life at H.M.S. Royal Arthur and the basic training at the outset. Everything seems so relaxed. David Lee and I have been assigned to work together driving the refuelling Bowser for the aircraft. How lucky to have David, who is much more practical and quite versed in engineering, but we get on well together.

We have to go with this huge tanker holding the fuel for the planes. David drives, I'm his mate. My duty is to plug a probe into the ground which acts as an earth. Goodness knows why that's needed, but it is! Then a little motor drives a pump that pushes the fuel into the tanks of the plane.

We have to be very, very careful to avoid spillage.

When we are not engaged in these duties we look after camp bicycles which are a very useful and quick form of transport around the large airfield. David does the more skilled operations, like fixing the brake blocks and mending punctures. I am quite happy doing the most necessary of tasks – cleaning the bikes and oiling the chains and wheels. We are under no pressure at all. We work in a small workshop adjacent to a huge hanger.

Next to us are some regular Royal Navy skilled air fitters, most of them leading hands. In charge of us all is a Chief Petty Officer. He seems much older, but I suppose he's under 40 years. He is short and barrel shaped, hence his nickname, Kettle-belly. One of the few who uses moderate language, he treats David Lee and me in a kindly way. When we first turned up to H.M.S. Hornbill he said, "You boys want time to settle in, so take two day-makers." That is short for 'make and mend', i.e. two days to do as you like.

So we sorted our kit out in the billet. Two spacious areas in a brick dormitory. Single beds with large lockers and a small table, and bathroom and shower room adjoining. It's like living in a hotel compared to other stations we'd been posted to.

Then David and I spent the rest of the two days looking round the camp, swimming in the station's pool and playing tennis and bowls. What a life!

We get a long weekend leave every two weeks from Friday night till midnight on Sunday.

The other weekend Kettle-belly told us, "You are free from Saturday 1400 hours (2pm) till midnight Sunday night. What you do then, I don't give a damn!"

So we walked to the far side of the camp perimeter track, got through a dry ditch and hedge and made our way to Beccles.

Mostly we get a lift into Fakenham and will hitch our way home. Drivers will gladly pick up a sailor in uniform and the greeting 'Where you going Jack?' is common. Often it's one of Leggett's lorries going home from Norwich market. Some of those drivers know me. As I know I'll be home again each weekend I save money by staying on the camp all week. Look forward to seeing you in the Summer. Thanks for your visits to my parents, they appreciate it a lot I know.

As ever,

David

Mr Philip Ashford was an early mentor of mine when I worked on his farm as a pupil in the Waveney Valley.

BECCLES
WEEKEND LEAVE
LATE SEPTEMBER 1949

Dear Mr Ashford,

It was good to meet you near the Corn Hall in Beccles when I was home on leave from West Raynham. How nice of you to say that I can have a couple of weeks work at the farm whilst on demob leave, before I go to college in October. A little extra cash will be handy.

I have enjoyed my time in the Navy and would not have missed it for anything. I have met some splendid folk and had some exciting times. But it will be good to be back in East Anglia and involved with farming again.

Did you read in the paper that the King visited the station a few weeks ago. It was quite an event. Everyone had to be extra smart in our uniforms and the boots had an extra polish. There was a big parade of the R.A.F. chaps, but as the Senior Service us few Naval boys led the parade. Felt proud marching behind the band.

It will be good to be back on the farm for a couple of weeks. The harvest will be over, but I may be able to help pruning the blackcurrants. It will be interesting to see if the horses remember me; I bet Aldeby Darlin' will.

Again, thank you for your help,

Best wishes,

David Woodward

In my 60s, nearly half a century after the events described in these letters, I studied for an Open University degree. Robert Massey was my tutor; we have kept in touch ever since.

MAY 2012
FROSTENDEN

Dear Robert,

I was very interested that you wanted to know how National Service had affected and changed my life. It certainly changed it a lot. You may remember me saying that one of the courses I took, when I was studying for my OU degree some years ago, enabled me to focus on the benefits of my short time in the Navy and likewise the things that were not so good. It was a course that looked at the effects of networks and hierarchies: and my goodness the Royal Navy at the time was riddled with both.

Our initial square-bashing made the whole hierarchical structure of the camp so apparent. But in response to this, all we new entrants formed our own networks, so we could cope with this new and strange way of having to live. We thought the discipline, especially on the parade ground, but also in the sporting activities, was pretty stupid: you had to obey commands without question. But then later, when I worked on the flight deck of an aircraft carrier, I came to realise that men's lives could well depend on the speed at which orders were carried out – and unquestioningly carried out. Because of this, I think a short period of National Service, not necessarily in the armed services, would be good for young people today.

Over the years I have become aware of what I would regard as the futility of war, but at the time, all those years ago, I was certain that I wanted to 'join up' and serve my country. Because I worked in agriculture I could have avoided doing National Service, but I had no wish to do so. I had set my heart on the

Royal Navy, and I knew that if I applied for early call-up, at seventeen and a half, I stood a better chance of this. I always had a hankering for the Navy; I liked the sea and open air. And all the nice girls loved a sailor, as I was soon to find out on shore leave.

But, apart from that, what an education National Service gave us. You came in touch with so many different folk from all around the country, people you would otherwise never meet. And also, older veterans who had survived the war. I now wish, with hindsight, that I had used the opportunity to have talked more to them, in depth rather than in brief snippets of conversation.

Working on the flight deck I also witnessed acts of great skill and bravery. And on one occasion became only too aware of death, and of how grief at the loss of comrades can bring shipmates of all ranks together.

I certainly benefited from my brief spell in the Navy. And all through my life I have experienced kindness and comradeship that all ex-Navy folk have extended to me, even to this day. I hope and trust that I have returned a little also myself.

In short, I would say that National Service provided me with a learning process that was equal to any lecture I ever attended.

Sixty-plus was a good age to study for a B.A. It was so good to learn for fun, and not with the aim of getting on in the world. And the reason I got through the examinations was because I never worried about failing. Maybe my tutors played a part also!

Thank you, Robert,
my best wishes to you and your family
David

Tribute to Commander Courage

I don't think I had more than a total of two hours conversation with a Comminsioned Officer all the time I was in the Navy, and that was often a brief 'Aye, aye Sir!' But I did get to know some of them and without a doubt the one who made a great impression and lasting memory was Commander Courage as executive officer on the Illustrious in 1948 to 1949 which coincided with the period I was on the ship.

In the *Daily Telegraph* Obituary after his death in 1998 at the age of 88 he was described as the most genial of men and had "a great rapport with the sailors in every ship he served in" Certainly so when I was on the ILLUSTRIOUS. When the voice came over the tannoy – "This is the Commander speaking" – there would be a hush as we listened to the man who truly lived up to the name of Richard Courage. Often this was in the Dog Watches – around teatime when we were all gathered in the mess deck, if we were not at sea or engaged in flying trials or exercises. Then the day was finished and were able to relax and listen.

He had the manner of a skilled radio presenter who made you feel it was just you he was talking to. He would tell us, as far as he was able to, what the programme ahead of us would be. At the time of the Liberty Boat disaster he also kept us up to date with whatever information there was concerning the progress of the survivors.

He chose to specialise as a signal officer in the hope it would enable him to go sailing. His Army racing friends tried to get him to transfer. But no chance he said "I absolutely love the Navy and anyway I only do it to beat the Army"

Commander Courage served in the carrier LONDON at the time of the Abyssinian Crises and the Spanish Civil War. He also saw much service during the war in SCYLLA, the flagship of Rear Admiral Rob Burnett. Often they would go through over 24 hours without sleep but he and his staff never faltered. He was awarded the Distinguished Service Cross.

Later in the war he was on the flag-bridge on the DUKE OF YORK when ships of the home fleet hunted down and sank the German battle cruiser SCHARNHORST off Norway on Boxing day 1943. In 1944 when British ships were to operate with the American Navy. Richard Courage carried out the difficult and complicated task to change the fleets signalling methods to the American method.

He was a brave, clever and kind man. I'm grateful he was Commander on the ILLUSTRIOUS in the short time I served on the ship.

To David Lee, Vic Smart and all old Illustrious ship mates

David Lee and I developed a friendship in 1949 that lasts to this day. I stopped him from spewing into the wind when he was overcome with sea-sickness. We discovered soon after that our respective homes in Suffolk were only about two miles apart, yet we had never met before.

Vic Smart, a fellow mess mate, was a regular sailor who looked after us young National Service boys. He was our mentor, Cox'n of the Captain's Barge and also a Royal Navy boxing champion – a useful chap to have on your side.

* * * * *

Dear Shipmates

This is my final letter about National Service on board HMS Illustrious.

I do not know if service in any other of the armed forces would have had the same impact on the rest of my life, but I think not. It is over 70 years since Vic Smart, David Lee and I were in the same mess and Victor Smart looked after us young National Servicemen. Woe betide any senior rating who appeared in his eyes to be bullying us.

One thing that surprised and pleased me over the years is that although my time in the Navy was short, it was a period of my life I have never forgotten.

I can think of many times in my later life when the moment someone heard that I was ex-Navy, I would immediately be treated as a shipmate.

I'll give you an example: a retired Naval Commander lived near us, and whenever trees were cut down on his land, a load of logs would arrive for our wood burner. And again: I was once made redundant and one of the Directors of the firm made sure

I was given free-lance work to supplement my unemployment benefit – he was ex-Navy.

When I became a Civil Servant, three former Navy men who were on the staff helped me enormously and guided me through the strange pattern of Civil Service Codes. And even now, when I find myself in need of advice or care, my ex-Navy connections are still fruitful.

So, thank you HMS Illustrious for letting me serve on your flight deck, albeit only for ten months.

Yours aye

David Woodward LFX 852205